W9-BWK-942

EDITED BY HELEN EXLEY
ILLUSTRATED BY JULIETTE CLARKE

Published simultaneously in 1999 by Helen Exley Giftbooks in Grea
Britain, and Helen Exley Giftbooks LLC in the USA.
Copyright © Helen Exley 1999
The moral right of the author has been asserted.

12 11 10

ISBN 1-86187-131-7

A copy of the CIP data is available from the British Library. All right
reserved. No part of this publication may be reproduced in any form
Printed in China.

Helen Exley Giftbooks, 16 Chalk Hill, Watford, Herts WD19 4BG, UK.
Helen Exley Giftbooks LLC, 185 Main Street, Spencer, MA 01562, USA.
www.helenexleygiftbooks.com

The publishers are grateful for permission to reproduce copyright material. Whilst every
reasonable effort has been made to trace copyright holders, the publishers would be pleased
hear from any not here acknowledged. Barbara Alpert: From "No Friend Like A Sister" Ed.
Alpert published Berkley Books © 1996 B. Alpert. Dirk Bogarde: From "An Orderly Man"
published Chatto and Windus © 1983 Labofilms S.A. Reprinted permission of Alfred A
Knopf Inc. and Random House UK Ltd. Polly Devlin: From "All Of Us There" published
Blackstaff Press © 1983 Polly Devlin. Reprinted by permission of the author. Elizabeth Fis
From "Sisters" © 1997 Elisabeth Fishel. Reprinted by permission of Conari Press. Toni
McNaron: Reprinted by permission of the publisher from McNaron, T.A.H. (Ed.) "The Sis
Bond" (New York: Teachers College Press © 1985 Teachers College, Columbia University.
rights reserved.) Virginia Woolf: From "The Letters of Virginia Woolf", Volume VI 1936-
1941 © 1980 Quentin Bell and Angela Garnett published by Harcourt Brace & Company
The Hogarth Press. PAM BROWN, PAMELA DUGDALE, CHARLOTTE GRAY, LISET
FAVIER, STUART & LINDA MACFARLANE, MAYA V PATEL, HELEN THOMSON,
TARA WOODS: published with permission © Helen Exley 1999.

I know that whatever
the disaster I blunder into,
you will rescue me.
Pausing only to tell me
what an idiot I've been.

NEVER ALONE

No matter the problem.

No matter the pain.

No matter the years that pass

Sisters will always be there.

STUART AND
LINDA
MACFARLANE

Having a sister means never being alone in life.

LINDA MACFARLANE

I have arrived at their doorsteps in complete need at various junctures of my life, and they have always, unconditionally been there for me.

CAROL WINCENC
ON HER SISTERS JANA AND LINDA

The applause of a sister means far more than that of any crowd. For she sees your achievement. She sees all that led up to it.

PAM BROWN, b.1928

HAVING A SISTER,

HOWEVER FAR OFF

MAKES THE

WORLD LESS LONELY.

PAMELA DUGDALE

She is... my touchstone, my idol, my light, and my sunshine. My life would be dark without her.

MARY ABBAJAY

... her paintings have made every place I have lived in my home.

MARGARET MEAD
(1901–1978),
ON HER SISTER ELIZABETH

TO THE RESCUE!

Sisters can Deal with
the man who has
left you flat on your face.
He will never forget her
as long as he lives!

. . .

A sister defending a sibling
is a fearsome sight.

. . .

It's remarkable what
a powerful left hook
your fragile sister has
when it comes to
your defence.

PAM BROWN, b.1928

Sisters don't need
careful explanations.
They don't even need
full sentences....

PAMELA DUGDALE

Sisters sometimes talk about
how they can see through
each other, never misled by
the other's pretences,
instinctively knowing
the other's true feelings.

TARA WOODS

OUR TIMES

SISTERS ARE OUR PEERS,

THE VOICE OF

OUR TIMES.

ELIZABETH FISHEL,
FROM "SISTERS"

To the outside world they
are two very, very old ladies.
To each other they are Ivy
and Rose,
their childhood close
behind them,
their memories bright.

CHARLOTTE GRAY, b.1937

WHEN SHE CAME IN, IT WAS LIKE THE SUN STREAMING INTO THE ROOM.

NANCY LANGHORNE,
LATER LADY ASTOR

MY SISTER'S VOICE

I have always loved my sister's voice. It is clear and light, a voice without seasons, like bells over a green city or snowfall on the roots of orchids. Her voice is a greening thing, an enemy of storm and dark and winter.

TOM WINGO,
FOR HIS TWIN SISTER SAVANNAH

BABY SISTER

The baby gazes enraptured at her
sister, watching her draw and write,
make faces, dance for her.
The six year old cradles her, kisses her,
winds the music box. Reads her
stories, delights in this new treasure
her own, her very own dear sister.

PAM BROWN, b.1928

In the woods, you suddenly feel a
little hand take yours
— and you know you could take on
any dragon that you chance to meet.

. . .

The only person I'm prepared to
make duck noises for,
and crawl like a crocodile,
and sing to,
and read the Three Bears for
the fifty-fifth time —
is my littlest sister.

PAM BROWN, b.1928

Uses of a Sister

Little sisters are useful
for tying to stakes.
Also for going back
to the house to fetch things
you've forgotten.
And steadying nails
for the hammer.

A big sister is always useful
— as a horse
— as a turner of ropes
— as a singer to sleep
— as a keeper of secrets.
And the pay is good
— a hug and a kiss
and a drowsy goodnight.

CHARLOTTE GRAY, b.1937

Life is never dull with a sister

CHAOS!

To have sisters
is to be involved in
an ongoing soap opera.

. . .

Bedlam is a household
of sisters getting ready
to go out for the evening.

PAM BROWN, b.1928

Unrelated images rush through my mind when I think of my kid sister: a vision in smeared lipstick, clopping around in my high heels; her tears the night before my wedding when she was feeling deserted.... Her courage in the face of tough campaigns, her integrity, her smarts, all laced with a large dose of humor and a willingness to be there for family are the qualities which fill me with pride and joy in such a sister.

FRANCES HALPERN,
ON HER SISTER LORETTA
WEINBERG, NEW JERSEY
ASSEMBLYWOMAN

Here we were together, talking to each other as we had in the days of childhood. Comfortable in each other's company, knowing it so well, trusting it so deeply, relaxed, continuing. Aware that we knew each other better than perhaps anyone else would ever do.

DIRK BOGARDE

SHE KNOWS YOU TOO WELL

Eyes turn – you wear gold
lamé like a second skin.
... Your sister knows your
bra is held up
with a safety pin.

. . .

Sisters know all your best
stories better than you.
And are inclined to put
you right.

PAM BROWN, b.1928

Dear Mum

I am writing to you to ask you if you could make my sister be quiet for a few seconds. Now I see why her nickname is Foghorn Fanny, with her loud music. I don't mind you teaching her drama, but could you make her a miming expert — you know, the stuff without words....

Love from Robbie

ROBBIE JARVIS, AGED 7

BRIDGED BY LOVE

... the gaps between us were too big to cross by efforts at rational thought. They were only bridged by love, by seeking to forgive, by consolation, by each sister

revealing painfully that she
was as human and
vulnerable as the other, and
by being accommodated at
such moments by the other.

POLLY DEVLIN

WHO GOT THE BLAME?

Who tied ribbons on the cat's tail?
Who used Dad's tie to make teddy a coat?
Who flooded the house while
bathing her dolls?
Who frightened Grandma by putting
spiders in the bath?
ME!
Who got the blame?
My sister.
That's what sisters are for!!!

STUART MACFARLAN

THE HORRIBLE TRUTH

Who applauds your
successes — but makes
quite sure you don't let 'em
go to your head?

CHARLOTTE GRAY, b.1937

Sisters are the best
people to have with you
when you're shopping
for clothes.
They tell you the truth.

PAM BROWN, b.1928

BIG SISTERS ARE THE CRAB GRASS
IN THE LAWN OF LIFE.

CHARLES M. SCHULZ, b.1922

It's a terrible thing being
a second girl.
The reason your mother
is so delighted at your birth
is because you can wear
all your elder sister's
hand-me-downs.

PAM BROWN, b.1928

LOYALTY

A sister will tell you how
charming and handsome
your new boyfriend is.
Then two weeks later when
he dumps you she will
tell you how stupid and
ugly he was.

LINDA MACFARLANE

Your sister will be
the first to criticise you
but if anyone else tries to,
your sister will defend
you until the end of
the world.

LISETTE FAVIER

TALK, TALK, TALK

We kick off our shoes, unloosen belts
and buttons, raid the fridge, sprawl by
the fire and talk and talk. And talk.

MAYA V. PATEL, b.194³

Sophisticated sisters, long apart,
can turn into giggly school girls
over just one cup of coffee.

PAM BROWN, b.192

TOGETHER AGAIN

... suddenly seeing her walk through the door towards me. There'd be a burst and a huge hug and a great amount of giggling... enormous delight in seeing each other again.

HILARY DU PRÉ,
ON HER SISTER JACQUELINE

Every now and then our arms
would fly around each other
in a hug and we'd look in each
other's eyes and say how
happy we were.

BERNIECE BAKER MIRACLE,
SISTER OF MARILYN MONROE

My sister Mary – best friend, soul mate, business partner – inspires me, awes me, encourages me. She is the first person I turn to in times of trouble, in times of joy.... Though we work together and live three blocks apart, we must speak at least twice a day on the phone. My boyfriend and her husband just don't get it. We do – we're sisters.

STEPHANIE ABBAJAY

MISSING EACH OTHER

You can't think how I depend upon you, and when you're not there the colour goes out of my life, as water from a sponge; and I merely exist, dry and dusty.

VIRGINIA WOOLF (1881-1941)
TO VANESSA BELL

And with no one to speak to, of what I felt, no Jane to comfort me and say that I had not been so very weak and vain and nonsensical as I knew I had! Oh! how I wanted you!

JANE AUSTEN (1775-1817), FROM "PRIDE AND PREJUDICE"

A sister is someone who knows where you stow your chocolate, all your secrets — and yet only occasionally blackmails you

STUART AND LINDA
MACFARLAN

Your secrets are her secrets.
Her stockings are your
stockings.
And you give and take the
sort of advice on clothes,
cash, spots and boyfriends
that no other member of the
family would dare.

VICTORIA BARCLAY, FROM "DAILY
MAIL", AUGUST 4TH, 1987

BOSSY BIG SISTER!

Grown-up elder sisters
still have this built-in instinct
to blow your nose
and pull up your socks.

PAMELA DUGDALE

Big sisters take you to
the cinema if parents
nag enough.
But never to what you
wanted to see.
Like "The Slimeball from
the Pit".

PAM BROWN, b.1928

MEMORIES

"Do you remember?" Brings back those summer skies, the sweet, high song of larks, the waist-high grasses. Sweets stuck to their disintegrating paper bags. The blank wall chalked with goals and targets. Alone, it is but half emembered. Together, we still feel he clutch of each other's hands as ve run from shouting boys or narling dogs. Together, we sit at he top of the darkened stairs and isten to the voices of the grown-ps. Together, we are on certain round.

PAM BROWN, b.1928

Husbands of sisters
escape on the golf course
while their wives
relive their childhood.

CHARLOTTE GRAY, b. 1937

I heard her first cry.
I gave her her first doll.

I held her hand on her first
day at school.
I beat off the school bully
when he made her sad.

We grew up together and
grew into friends.

Now she's all grown up and
can look after herself.
But I'll always be there, just
in case.
'Cos she's my baby sister.

LINDA MACFARLANE

No matter how much we disagree, I cannot close the book on my sister.

TONI McNARON,
FROM "THE SISTER BOND"

If you tell your sister to go to hell in twelve different languages and you need a quarter, you can say, "I need a quarter". And she'll give it to you. A friend may say, I don't want to see you again.

ELIZABETH MEAD STEIG

REMEMBERING

Sisters remember.
The birthday when you broke
your leg.
The visit to the zoo when you
wouldn't leave the warthog.
The time you broke that vase,
– and fixed it with tape.
The time you turned up at the

wrong birthday party. The Sunday
you set off for school. The day you
won the cup.
Others forget –
but siblings
remember. Forever.

PAM BROWN, b.1928

We have been friends together,
in sunshine and in shade;
since first beneath the chestnut
trees, in infancy we played.

CAROLINE NORTON

...THAT CHILDISH WORLD

... we never found again
That childish world where our
two spirits mingled
Like scents from varying roses
that remain
One sweetness....

GEORGE ELIOT
(MARY ANN EVANS) (1819-1880)

IN TIMES OF CRISIS

Sometimes I dread waking
up to a big crisis – then
I cheer up because
Little Sister will be there
to give me excellent advice.

JESSICA MARTIN, FROM
"DAILY MAIL", AUGUST 4TH, 1987

I had just come out of
a coma when she... leaned
over my bed and whispered,
"Little Mich, little Mich,
don't you worry about
anything. Wherever I go,
I'll take care of you."
And she has.

MICHIE NADER

It took years for us
to find our own pace,
to create a silence
in which to hear only
the sound of our own footsteps
and not feel that the silence
was a lonely emptiness.

POLLY DEVLIN

Late at night, coming home from holiday dinners at our aunt's home just hours after one of our quarrels, my eyelids would become heavy and I'd snuggle next to Daryl and rest my head on her lap. The imaginary dividing line forgotten, she would gently stroke my hair and twirl my ponytail, and often I would feel so close to her that I'd try to fight off sleep to savor the moment. My big sister was taking care of me.

DR. DALE V. ATKINS, FROM "SISTERS"

SIX GOING ON SIXTY

Even when you
are sixty,
you are still six
to your sister.

PAM BROWN, b.1928

Only a sister can compare the sleek body that now exists with the chubby body hidden underneath. Only a sister knows about former pimples, failing math, and underwear kicked under the bed.

LAURA TRACY,
FROM "THE SECRET BETWEEN US"

A sister is your finest guide
Escorting you along unfamiliar paths
Supporting you each time you stumble
Encouraging you when the way is hard
Congratulating you when you reach
your destination.
Always with you
wherever you choose to go.

STUART AND LINDA MACFARLANE

THE REASON
I AM LIVING

Neither one of us ever
married and we've lived
together most all of our lives,
and probably know each other
better than any two human
beings on Earth. After so long,

To Judy —

8/26/07

SISTERS!
A LITTLE GIFTBOOK

A HELEN EXLEY GIFTBOOK

EXLEY
NEW YORK • WATFORD, UK

From Erin

YOUR WITNESS

She is your witness, who sees
you at your worst and best, and
loves you anyway. She is your
partner in crime, your
midnight companion, someone
who knows when you are
smiling, even in the dark.

BARBARA ALPERT

we are in some ways like one person. She is my right arm. If she were to die first, I'm not sure if I would want to go on living because the reason I am living is to keep her living.

SADIE DELANY, AGED 103, ABOUT HER SISTER BESSIE, AGED 101

WE DANCED IN PUDDLES...

We danced in puddles, we sang in the rain.
We skipped in the park, we kicked
up the leaves.

We got up to mischief, we played all
sorts of tricks.
We share a history no one else can share.
My sister and I.

STUART AND LINDA MACFARLANE

LIFE PASSAGES

As in so many ways life passages
behind us and ahead of us,
we've become reference points
for each other, lodestars for each
other, as we separate and cross
paths again.

ELIZABETH FISHEL

You and I were and are and will
be forever friends.
Despite all differences.
Despite all change.

PAM BROWN, b.1928

Sisters.

Yes, we're just sisters.
Our story is not heroic,
not even memorable.
But when I need support
I sense you quietly by me.
I always will.

HELEN THOMSON, b.1943